TESLA

By Jennifer Colby

45TH PARALLEL PRESS

Published in the United States of America by Cherry Lake Publishing Group
Ann Arbor, Michigan
www.cherrylakepublishing.com

Reading Adviser: Beth Walker Gambro, MS Ed., Reading Consultant, Yorkville, IL
Book Designer: Jen Wahi

Photo Credits: © Yauhen_D/Shutterstock, cover, 1; © Darren Brode/Shutterstock, 4; © canadianPhotographer56/Shutterstock, 6, 7, 12; © ilikeyellow/Shutterstock, 8; © Jonathan Weiss/Shutterstock, 10, 11; © Oleksandr Grechin/Shutterstock, 13; © Mike Mareen/Shutterstock, 14, 29; © vicy/Alamy Stock Photo, 17; © Sergio Azenha/Alamy Stock Photo, 17; © UPI/Alamy Stock Photo, 18, 19; © Artoholics/Shutterstock, 20; © TonelsonProductions/Shutterstock, 21; © PR images/Alamy Stock Photo, 22; © agefotostock /Alamy Stock Photo, 24; © Kaspars Grinvalds/Shutterstock, 27; © Kathy Hutchins/Shutterstock, 30; © Grzegorz Czapski/Shutterstock, 31; © William Barton/Shutterstock, 31.

45th Parallel Press is an imprint of Cherry Lake Publishing Group.

Library of Congress Cataloging-in-Publication Data

Names: Colby, Jennifer, 1971- author.
Title: Tesla / by Jennifer Colby.
Description: Ann Arbor, Michigan : Cherry Lake Publishing, [2022] | Series:
  Floored! Supercars
Identifiers: LCCN 2022005377 | ISBN 9781668909515 (hardcover) | ISBN
  9781668911112 (paperback) | ISBN 9781668912706 (ebook) | ISBN
  9781668914298 (pdf)
Subjects: LCSH: Tesla automobiles--Juvenile literature. | Sports
  cars--Juvenile literature.
Classification: LCC TL215.T43 C65 2022 | DDC 629.222/2--dc23/eng/20220216
LC record available at https://lccn.loc.gov/2022005377

Printed in the United States of America by
Corporate Graphics

ABOUT THE AUTHOR:

Jennifer Colby is a school librarian in Ann Arbor, Michigan. She does not drive a supercar, but she likes going to auto shows to see what they look like.

Table of Contents

One place to see a Tesla supercar is at an auto show or in a showroom.

CHAPTER 1
What Are Supercars?

Cars get us where we need to go. We drive them to school and work. We drive them to the grocery store or a friend's house. If we need to go someplace, a car can get us there. But some people want a car that is more than a way to get around. They want a car with high **performance**, **luxury**, or **technological** features. Performance is how well something works. Luxury means great comfort. Technological means using science and engineering. These car owners want to drive a **supercar**.

A supercar is a sports car. It is designed to provide a high-level driving experience. Drivers of supercars expect excellent **acceleration**, **handling**, and **maneuvering**. Acceleration is the act of moving faster. Handling is the way a car moves when it is driven. Maneuvering is a skillful way of moving.

Supercars are also known for their unique looks. You might see one of these eye-catching cars and admire it.

Have you seen a Tesla driving down the road? If so, then you have seen a supercar! What makes these cars so special?

Let's find out more about Teslas.

Teslas run on electric motors.

The Tesla logo is designed to look like an electric motor.

CHAPTER 2

Tesla History

Tesla, Inc. is a very new car company. It was founded in 2003 with a focus on manufacturing all-electric cars. If you drive a Tesla, you never have to stop at the gas station again.

A Tesla uses a large battery pack to run its electric motor. It needs to be charged on a regular basis. Electric motors make Teslas some of the most environmentally friendly cars on the road. They do not create fumes that pollute the air.

Tesla makes 4 car models. These are the Model S, Model X, Model 3, and Model Y. Teslas are very popular. They have become the fastest-growing car company in the world.

An **electric vehicle** needs to have its battery charged in order to run. Tesla owners can use a home **charging station** or find one somewhere else. A charging station is a piece of equipment that supplies electrical power for electric cars.

Different kinds of charging stations supply different amounts of power. The amount of power determines how long it will take to charge the car's batteries. An at-home charger will take several hours to fully charge a car. A Tesla Supercharger takes around 15 minutes to charge a car that can drive for about 200 miles (322 kilometers).

A Tesla plugged into a Supercharger.

Women helped design the Tesla Model X.

Behind the Wheel

The world of car design includes a lot of men. But many women design cars as well. A team of women worked on the design of the 2014 Tesla Model X. One of the lead designers was Kimberly Martes. She is a color, material, and **trend** specialist. Trends are things that are currently popular. Designers like Martes are aware of current design and color trends. They usually have a formal education in industrial or graphic design. Did you know you can get a college degree to become a color, material, and trend specialist?

The Tesla Model X was designed with the female driver in mind. Martes worked with other female designers on the team to choose the materials that gave the car a specific look and feel.

The 2009 cutting-edge Tesla Roadster.

CHAPTER 3
Tesla Evolution

Many people have tried to manufacture an all-electric vehicle. The first electric vehicles were made in the 1830s. Some were more successful than others. Many of these cars had low speeds, high costs, and short driving ranges. Tesla was the first company to design and produce an all-electric car that was **commercially** successful. Commercially means in a way that makes a profit.

Tesla's first all-electric car, the 2009 Roadster, was designed for speed, performance, and comfort. Today, the Tesla Model 3 is the world's best-selling all-electric car.

With no fuel line, tank, and other parts, a Tesla has a lot of extra space! Just like the back of the car, the front of a Tesla is a big trunk. Sometimes it is called a "frunk."

Frunk stands for "front trunk". The frunk is a very good **crumple zone**. A crumple zone is designed to bend easily in an accident. This protects the people inside.

The batteries and electric motors on a Tesla are underneath the car. This also makes the car very safe. Its low center of gravity helps prevent rollovers. Safety has always been important to Tesla. All Teslas come with outside cameras and sensors with a computer that can help the driver avoid accidents.

Tesla drivers can also expect great driving performance. With a top speed of 200 miles (322 km) per hour, the Tesla Model S Plaid can go from 0 to 60 miles (97 km) per hour in 1.99 seconds! It would take an average car more than 8 seconds to do the same! Just for fun, the Tesla has an in-car gaming system. It can be used only when the car is in park.

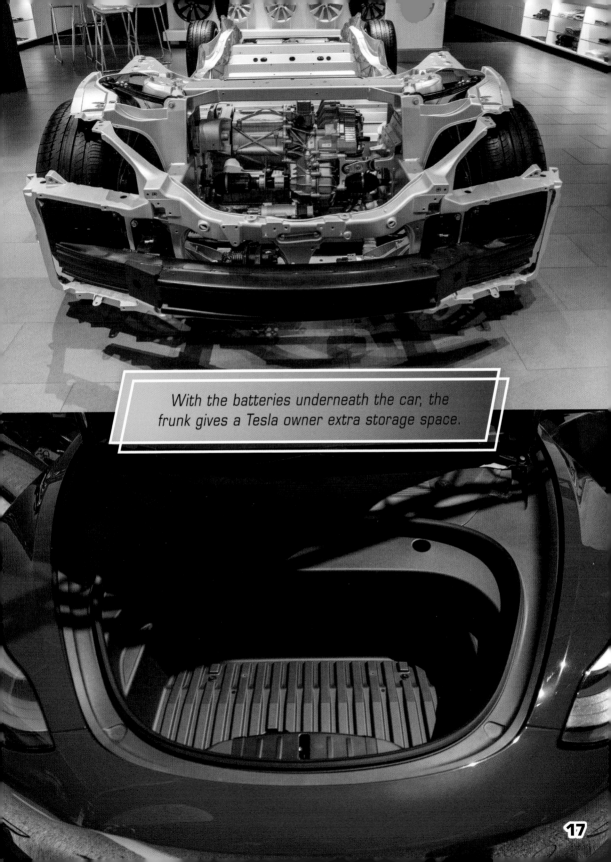

With the batteries underneath the car, the frunk gives a Tesla owner extra storage space.

SpaceX was founded in 2002.

Elon Musk helped develop Tesla, Inc. He also started a space exploration company called SpaceX. In 2018, SpaceX launched its Falcon Heavy test rocket. It took Musk's own 2010 Tesla Roadster into space! The Roadster is "driven" by a mannequin in a spacesuit. He is called "Starman."

A live-stream video of the launch ran for 4 hours. It was powered by the Roadster's batteries. Cameras attached to the car took images of Starman driving the Tesla as he was sent into **orbit**. The curved, invisible path that an object follows in space is its orbit.

SUSTAINABLE DESIGN

- The 2006 Tesla Roadster was the first successful modern all-electric vehicle.

- Tesla, Inc. produces 3 times more electrical power than all Tesla cars put together have used.

- In 2017, Tesla created the world's largest battery. It makes enough energy to power more than 30,000 homes.

- Tesla has set up 30,000 Superchargers worldwide.

- Emissions from creating electricity used to power electric cars are more than 22 percent lower than those of gasoline cars.

- In 2016, Tesla's factory in California was certified as a "Zero Waste" facility. That means it reuses or recycles all of its waste.

Tesla builds Supercharger stations, like these, around the world.

Tesla's space Roadster has already traveled almost 2 billion miles (3.2 billion km). Each orbit around the sun takes about 557 days. The Roadster moves at a speed of 52,394 miles (84,320 km) per hour. It has already "driven" more miles than any car on Earth. It has gone 56,634 times beyond its 36,000-mile (57,936 km) **warranty**. A warranty is a guarantee that a product will perform as promised for a certain amount of time. That's one special supercar!

You can track the path of the Tesla Roadster as it travels around the Sun. Many websites give updates about its location. The car has traveled far enough to drive all of the world's roads more than 51 times!

A 2010 Roadster is currently orbiting the Sun.

Which Tesla is your favorite?

CHAPTER 4

Tesla Today

Tesla car models can be custom ordered. Owners can choose paint color, interior color, and wheel style.

Tesla makes an affordable all-electric car. An entry-level Tesla Model 3 is $44,990. At $129,990, the highest-priced Tesla is the Model S Plaid. Every model has a touchscreen that controls everything in the car—even the glove compartment!

All Teslas also have self-driving options. For an extra $12,000, owners can choose a package that allows the car to navigate on autopilot. A Tesla can even change lanes and park automatically! The driver is still in charge. But the Tesla can do all the work.

All Teslas need their batteries charged. On a full charge, all Teslas can drive at least 262 miles (422 km). The range depends on how the car is driven. Faster speeds drain the battery more quickly. The Tesla Model S can go almost 400 miles (644 km) on one charge!

At home, it costs about $10.25 to fully charge the battery. Drivers have to pay to use a Tesla Supercharger. There are almost 1,200 Supercharger stations in the United States. Tesla drivers can go on any major highway in the United States and not have to worry about finding a place to charge. Depending on the time of day and the rate of charging, Tesla Superchargers cost about $7.20 to $11.20. Charging at a Tesla Supercharger is free for cars bought before January 2017.

Tesla made 2 of the top 10 best-selling electric cars in 2020.

Cost of Ownership

MODEL	PRICE
2021 Honda CRV	$25,350
2021 Ford Escape	$25,555
2021 Chevy Suburban	$52,300

MODEL	PRICE
2021 Tesla Model 3	$44,990
2021 Tesla Model Y Long Range	$58,990
2021 Tesla Model S	$94,990
2021 Tesla Model X Plaid	$119,990
2021 Tesla Model S Plaid	$129,990

Maintaining a Tesla is cheaper than maintaining a non-electric car. A Tesla does not need oil changes and never needs gasoline! The average Tesla owner spends about $282 per year to maintain the car. A non-electric car costs about $1,000 per year to maintain.

You will never see a Tesla at a gas station. But you will see them driving down the road. With the most popular all-electric car model in the world, Tesla is quickly becoming the supercar of electric vehicles!

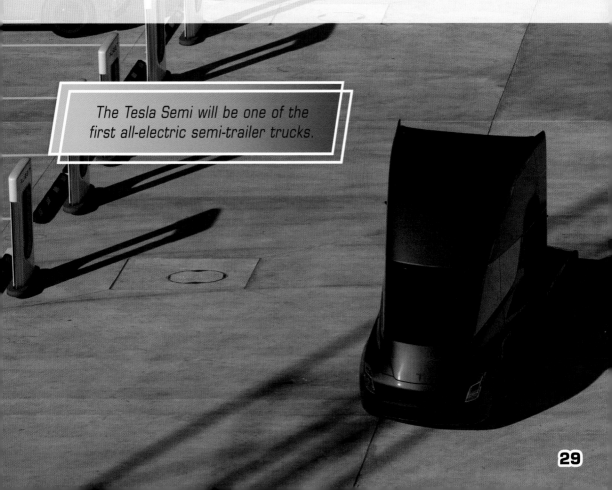

The Tesla Semi will be one of the first all-electric semi-trailer trucks.

Timeline of a Legend

Founding of Tesla, Inc.

2003

Tesla Roadster is produced

2008

2012

2004

Tesla Model S sedan is produced

Elon Musk becomes the chairman of Tesla, Inc.

■ Tesla Model X SUV
is produced

2015

■ Tesla Model Y crossover
is produced

2020

2021

2018

■ Tesla Model 3 becomes
all-time best-selling
plug-in electric car

■ A 2010 Tesla
Roadster is sent
into space

Find Out More

BOOKS

Great Lives in Graphics: Nikola Tesla. Lewes, United Kingdom: Button Books, 2022.

How Do Electric Motors Work? Physics Books for Kids. Newark, DE: Speedy Publishing, 2017.

WEBSITES

Kiddle—Tesla, Inc. Facts for Kids
https://kids.kiddle.co/Tesla,_Inc.

Where Is Starman?—Track Elon Musk's Tesla Roadster in Space!
https://www.whereisroadster.com

Glossary

acceleration (ik-seh-luh-RAY-shuhn) the act of moving faster

charging station (CHARJ-ing STAY-shuhn) a piece of equipment that supplies power for charging electric cars

commercially (kuh-MUR-shul-ee) related to the buying and selling of things

crumple zone (KRUHM-puhl ZOHN) the front part of a vehicle that is designed to bend easily in a crash

electric vehicle (ih-LEK-trik VEE-uh-kuhl) a car that uses an electric motor

handling (HAND-ling) the way a car moves when it is driven

luxury (LUHK-shuh-ree) great comfort and wealth

maneuvering (muh-NOO-vuh-ring) moving in a skillful way

orbit (OR-buht) curved path that something follows as it goes around something else

performance (puh-FOHR-muhns) how well something functions or works

supercar (SOO-puhr-kar) sports car designed for a high-level driving experience

technological (tek-nuh-LAH-jih-kuhl) relating to using science and engineering

trend (TREHND) something that is currently popular

warranty (WOHR-uhn-tee) a guarantee that a product will perform as promised for a certain amount of time

Index